THE MOON

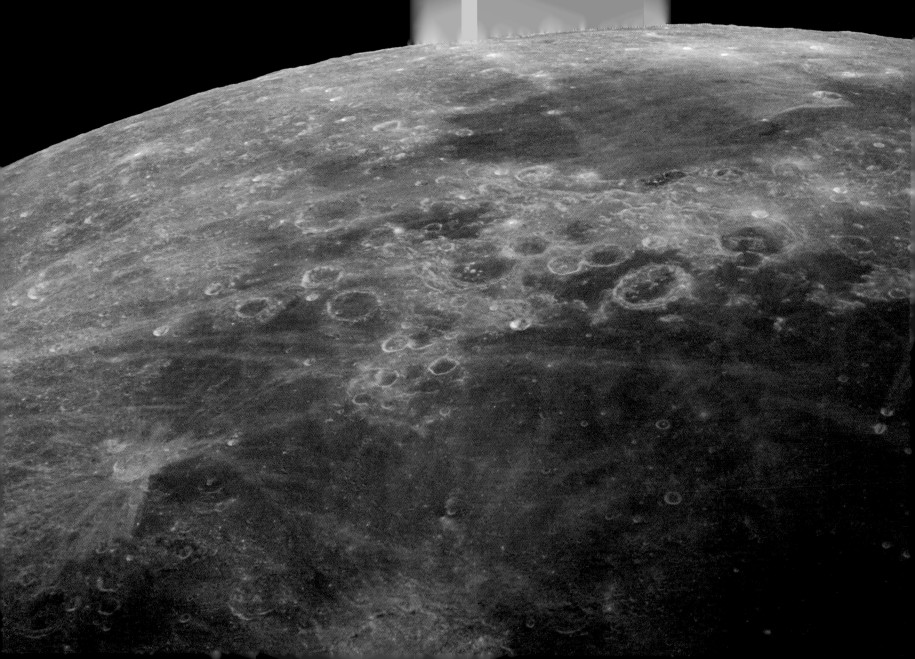

THE MOON

SEYMOUR SIMON

SIMON & SCHUSTER BOOKS FOR YOUNG READERS

New York   London   Toronto   Sydney   Singapore

SIMON & SCHUSTER BOOKS FOR YOUNG READERS
An imprint of Simon & Schuster Children's Publishing Division
1230 Avenue of the Americas, New York, New York 10020

SIMON & SCHUSTER BOOKS FOR YOUNG READERS is a trademark of
Simon & Schuster.
Book design by Mark Siegel
The text for this book is set in Goudy Old Style.
Photographs courtesy of NASA
Manufactured in Mexico
2   4   6   8   10   9   7   5   3   1
Library of Congress Cataloging-in-Publication Data
Simon, Seymour.
The moon / Seymour Simon.—Rev. ed.
p. cm.
ISBN 0-689-83563-9
1. Moon—Juvenile literature. 2. Moon—Photographs from space—Juvenile literature. [1. Moon.] I. Title.
QB582 .S545 2003
559.9'1—dc21   2001031303

Remembering my sister Roslyn

The moon is Earth's closest neighbor in space. It is about one quarter of a million miles away. In space that is very close.

The moon travels around Earth. It is Earth's only natural satellite. A satellite is an object that travels around another object. The moon takes about twenty-seven days and eight hours to go around the Earth once.

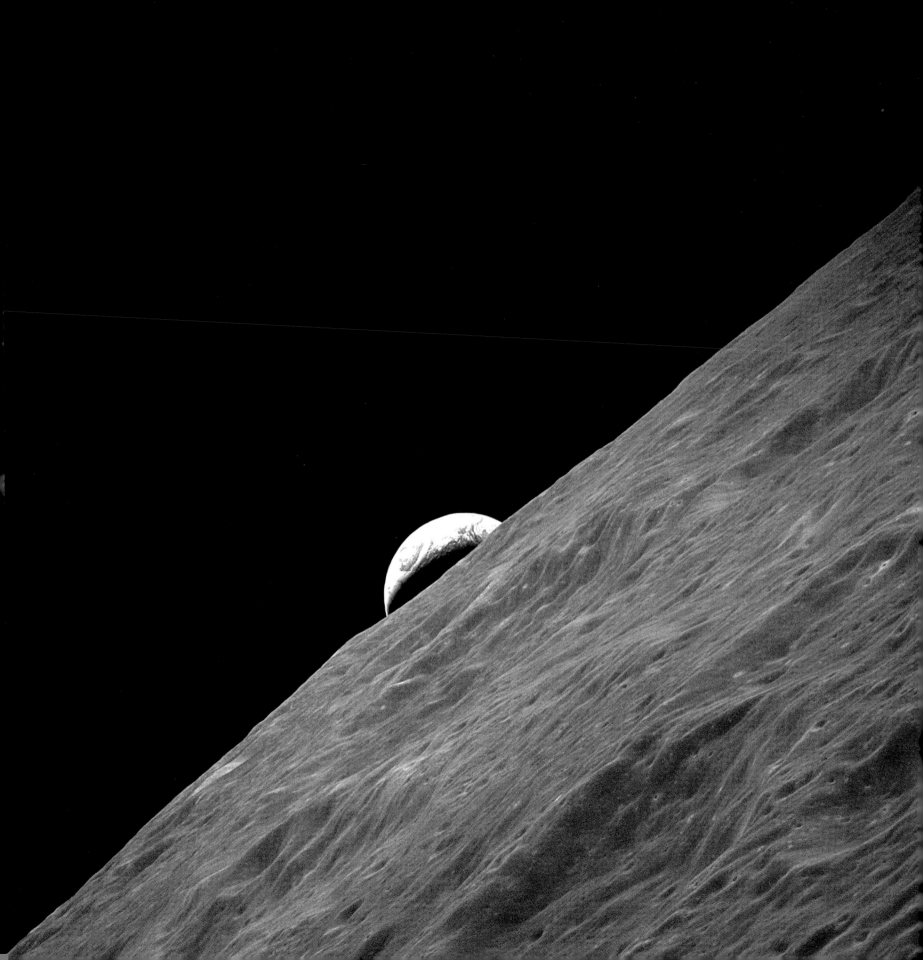

The moon is so close to the Earth that you can easily see light and dark on its surface. This photograph of the moon was taken through a telescope on Earth. The light places are mostly mountains and hills. The dark places are flatlands.

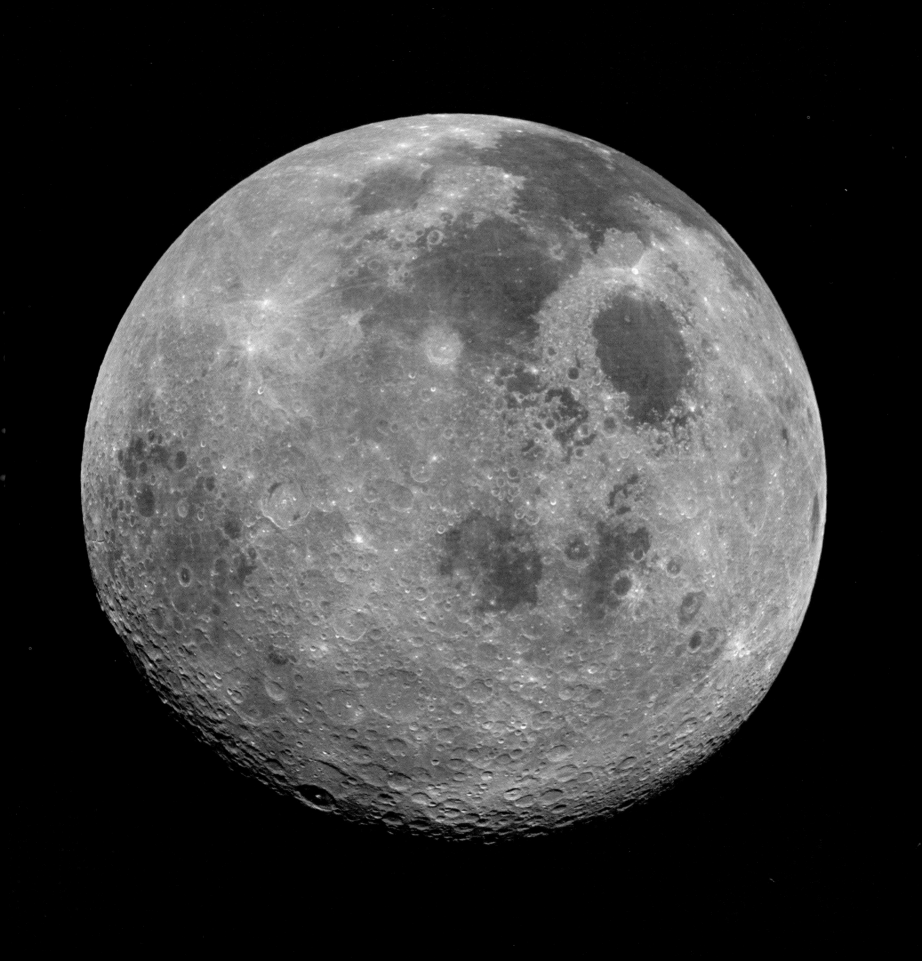

The moon has thousands of craters covering its surface. Craters are ring-shaped flatlands with walls around them. A few craters on the moon are more than fifty miles wide, but most are smaller. Many of the craters are only a few feet wide.

The moon is made of rock. We can see only part of the moon lit by sunlight. Sometimes we see the full moon. Other times we see a thin sliver. Every night the moon looks a little different. Each different shape is called a phase of the moon. The phases go all-dark, new moon through full moon, and back to new moon in about twenty-nine days. We call the phase in this photograph a crescent moon. From earliest times, people gazed up at the moon and wondered about it. Was the moon a world like ours? Were there living things on the moon? Would we ever be able to travel to the moon?

Over the years, scientists learned much about the moon by studying it from Earth with telescopes and other instruments. But many things were still unknown. Then in 1961, the United States government decided to try to send a person to the moon within ten years.

The space program was named Apollo. This photograph taken from the Apollo 11 *Columbia* spacecraft shows the lunar landing ship *Eagle* on its way back from the surface of the moon. The surface of the moon is visible sixty miles below the spacecraft. A quarter of a million miles away, a partly lit Earth hangs above the moon's horizon.

Before the space age, no one had ever seen the far side of the moon. That's because the same side of the moon always faces Earth. Then, space ships from Earth went around the moon. Here is one of the photographs taken from a spaceship. It shows parts of the moon's far side. You can see craters and mountains, much like those on the side of the moon we see from Earth. But the far side has few flat lands, or "seas."

On July 20, 1969, Neil Armstrong became the first person to set foot on the moon. Armstrong was one of the astronauts on the Apollo 11 flight to the moon. He was followed shortly by Edwin Aldrin, another member of the United States Apollo 11 space flight. This is a photograph of Astronaut Aldrin standing on the moon. The face mask of his space suit reflects Astronaut Armstrong.

This footprint on the moon marks the first time that human beings have walked on ground that was not Earth. The footprint may last for a million years or longer. That is because there is no air on the moon and without air, there can be no winds to blow dust around.

The astronauts could jump much higher on the moon than on Earth. People weigh much less on the moon than they do on Earth. The moon's gravity is one sixth that of the Earth's. Gravity causes objects to have weight. In places where there is less gravity, you weigh less and you can jump higher. That's why the astronauts could leap on the moon's surface. To find out what you would weigh on the moon, divide your weight by six.

The astronauts discovered that the moon is a silent, strange place. The moon has no air. Air carries sound. With no air, the moon is completely silent. Even when the astronauts broke rocks or used the rockets on their spaceship, sound could not be heard.

The sky on the moon is always black. On Earth, we can see stars only at night. On the moon, stars shine all the time.

39

The moon does not have air, water, clouds, rain, or snow. It does not have weather. But the surface of the moon does warm up or cool off. The ground gets very hot or very cold because there is no air to spread the heat. The temperatures in the daytime can be above the boiling point of water. At night, the temperature can drop hundreds of degrees below zero. The astronauts' space suits kept their bodies at the right temperature. The astronauts carried tanks on their backs that contained the air they needed for breathing.

Without air and water, the moon's surface has not worn away very much. The surface has changed so little that it holds clues to the early history of the moon. The astronauts searched for these clues. They collected rocks and brought them back to Earth for scientists to study. They set up instruments

Each Apollo crew brought back more information about the moon. The astronauts of Apollo 15 stayed nearly sixty-seven hours on the moon. They returned with 173 pounds of moon rocks and soil. Scientists all over the world studied the information the astronauts brought back. They learned that the moon is about the same age as Earth. But the moon's soil and rocks are different from Earth's. For instance, moon rocks contain no water at all, while almost all rocks on Earth contain a small amount of water.

Scientists also learned that many millions of years ago, the inside of the moon was hot enough to melt rock. Melted rock, or lava, spilled over the surface of the moon. The lava formed lakes and then hardened. The solid lava became dark flatlands. This is a photograph of flatlands on the moon. All of the small pits were made by rocks from space that hit the flatlands after they had hardened.

After millions of years, the inside of the moon cooled off. The lava stopped flowing. The moon then looked much as it does today. Its surface is covered with craters, mountains, valleys, and flatlands. There are very few changes on the moon today, but there are thousands of tiny moonquakes each year.

This is a photograph of a giant crater that is about fifty miles wide. The crater was formed when a huge rock from space crashed into the moon and buried itself. The rocks on the surface of the moon exploded. You can see the mountain peak that was formed in the center of the crater. The explosion also created the crater walls. Rocks and dust scattered for miles in all directions.

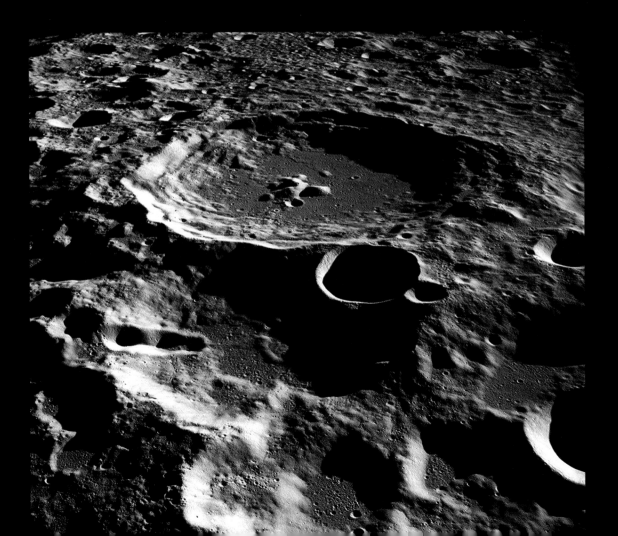

Apollo 17 was the last spaceship to carry people to the moon. It was launched in December 1972. The astronauts of Apollo 17 discovered the oldest rock ever found on the moon. Scientists on Earth tested the rock. They discovered that it was more than 4,500 million years old. They named it the Genesis rock. Before the astronauts returned to Earth, they left a plaque on the moon showing the history of moon travel. They also left a falcon feather and a four-leaf clover. The feather and the four-leaf clover stand for the living things of Earth.

Scientists have learned much about the moon from the Apollo space flights. They have found the answers to many questions they once had. For example, the moon rocks brought back by Apollo astronauts help explain how the moon was formed. Scientists think that long ago, the Earth collided in space with a very large object. They believe the moon formed from the material ejected from Earth during that collision. But in science, the questions never cease. Did the moon have water once? Did it ever have a magnetic field like Earth's? Much about the moon still remains a mystery.

Earth and its moon are close in space, but very different from each other. Earth is a blue, cloud-covered planet, filled with living things. The moon is a dead world. Without air or water, a cloud can never appear in its black sky and a raindrop will never fall.